MAKING
HEALTHY
FOOD
CHOICES

Food for Sports

Neil Morris

Customer Service 888-454-2279
Visit our website at
www.heinemannraintree.com

Designed by David Poole and Geoff Ward
Illustrations by Geoff Ward
Printed and bound in China by South China
Printing Company

10 09 08 07 06
10 9 8 7 6 5 4 3 2 1

**Library of Congress Cataloging-in-
Publication Data**
Morris, Neil, 1946-
  Food for sports / Neil Morris.-- 1st ed.
    p. cm. -- (Making healthy food
choices)
  Includes index.
  ISBN-13: 978-1-4034-8573-1 (hardback)
  ISBN-10: 1-4034-8573-9 (hardback)
  ISBN-13: 978-1-4034-8579-3 (pbk.)
  ISBN-10: 1-4034-8579-8 (pbk.)
  1. Nutrition--Juvenile literature. 2. Sports-
-Nutritional
aspects--Juvenile literature. I. Title. II.
Series.
  RA784.M6257 2006
  613.2--dc22
                          2006003971

Acknowledgments
The publishers would like to thank the
following for permission to reproduce
photographs: Action Plus Images pp.
36 (Erik Isakson), 38 (Mark Shearman);
Alamy Images p. 5 (Shotfile); Corbis
pp. 4 (Olivier Prevosto), 13 (Wolfgang
Rattay/Reuters), 15 (Joe McBride), 19 (Ron
Boardman; Frank Lane Picture Agency), 25
(Reuters/ Will Burgess), 26 (Tim de Waele),
34, 40 (Erich Schlegel/NewSport), 42
(Roger Ball), 51 top (Envision); Empics pp.
21 (AP Photo/ Paul Sakuma), 28 (PA/ RUI
VIEIRA), 39 (PA/ Rebecca Naden), 45 (AP/
MARKUS SCHREIBER); Getty Images pp. 7
(Christian Fischer/Bongarts), 8 (Stone/Jed
Share), 12 (AFP PHOTO/ FRANCK FIFE), 17
(Allsport Concepts), 18 (Photographer's
Choice/GSO Images), 22 (Photodisc), 23
(Botanica), 33 (Clive Brunskill), 35 (Bob
Martin), 43 (AFP PHOTO/ FRANCK FIFE),
46 (Doug Benc), 47 (Taxi/Ken Churnes), 49
(Taxi/ Tony Anderson); Harcourt Education
Ltd pp. 48 (MM Studios), 51 bott (MM
Studios); Photolibrary pp. 10 (Foodpix/
John E. Kelly), 14 (Foodpix/ Michael
Pohuski); Science Photo Library p. 24
(GUSTO PRODUCTIONS).

Cover photograph of Lance Armstrong
reproduced with permission of Getty
Images (AFP/Joel Saget)

The publishers would like to thank Nicole
Ann Clark RD for her assistance in the
preparation of this book.

CONTENTS

Any words appearing in the text in bold, **like this**,
are explained in the glossary.

ENERGY FOODS:
Fuel for Life

Most young people enjoy physical exercise in one form or another, and physical exercise is good for you. When you exercise, your body uses a lot of energy. This energy comes from the food you eat.

Food is energy for life. We use this energy all day, every day. When you run, jump, or take part in any kind of sports activity, your body has to perform at a high level. Your lungs work harder to take in oxygen. Your heart beats faster to pump oxygen around the body in your blood. Most importantly, your muscles burn fuel faster as they work hard to help you move.

▲ Athletes use up a huge amount of energy in a short period of time. This top-level sprinter put everything into her race.

The more active you are, the more energy you use and, generally, the more food you need. However, it is important to remember that young people do not need a special **diet** to take part in their favorite sports or to exercise. If you eat a healthy, **balanced diet**, your food should produce all the energy you need.

You might play a team game, like soccer or football, or take up an individual sport, such as cycling or running. If you take sports seriously and play for a school team or a club, you will know that it helps your performance to be fit. Part of keeping fit and healthy is making sure that you make the right choices about the food you eat and the fluids you drink. Food and drink provide us with the fuel we need for everything we do. Then you can enjoy your sport, which should be fun, at whatever level you play.

Eating sensibly and healthily is important even if you do not take part in competitive sports. Healthy eating is just as important for those who enjoy playing with friends in the park or taking a leisurely swim in the pool. We still need energy, and plenty of it.

▲ These players are taking a break from basketball to quench their thirst and replace lost fluids.

WHAT ELSE DOES FOOD DO FOR US?

In addition to giving us energy, food does other jobs. It provides us with substances that help build, repair, and replace **tissues** in our bones, muscles, and **organs**. These substances are needed to regulate our bodily processes and help make blood **cells**. They also help us to grow.

MEASURING ENERGY

Scientists usually measure the energy we get from food in units called **kilojoules** (**kJ**). Most athletes and people trying to lose weight use a different system of units, called **calories** (or cal). Since one calorie is a tiny amount of energy, people actually calculate in thousands of calories (called **kilocalories**, or kcal). To add to the confusion, they usually call these kilocalories "calories"! Most food labels give both measures of energy, but health books and magazine articles usually stick to calories. We will also use calories (kcal) in this book.

One kilocalorie is the same as about four kilojoules. To convert more precisely from one system to the other:
1 kcal (usually called a calorie) = 4.18 kJ or 1 kJ = 0.24 kcal.

The number of calories you need depends on many things, including your gender, height, weight, and fitness level. It is also affected by how much energy you use up, so exercise and sports will influence what and how much you need to eat. The chart below gives an average for different ages, but note that figures may vary.

We all use up energy at different rates. Boys usually burn more calories than girls because they generally have larger muscles that use more energy. Strenuous sports and activities use more energy than gentle ones.

Calorie burners

activity (for 30 minutes)	approximate calories (kcal) used
running	290
swimming	260
ice hockey	250
basketball	230
rowing machine	220
tennis	220
soccer	210
aerobics	200
jogging	200
cycling	190
badminton	180
baseball/softball	170
golf	130
riding horseback	130
weight-training	130
walking	110

How many calories (kcal) do you need per day?

age	girls/ women	boys/ men
7–10	1,740	1,970
11–14	1,845	2,220
15–18	2,110	2,755
19–50	1,940	2,550

WOW!

If you ate nothing, your glycogen stores would only last about a day OR be enough to run about 20 miles (32 kilometers).

▲ Soccer players need a lot of energy. This is a women's international match between Germany and the United States.

STORAGE TANKS

We need energy reserves for all activities, including sports. Otherwise we would have to keep eating most of the time, at the same rate that we use energy up. In fact we have a number of energy stores in our bodies.

Some food is turned into a substance called **glycogen**. The glycogen is stored in the liver and in muscles. People with large muscles store more glycogen. If you have a low amount of glycogen, you will tire more easily when you are active in your sport. This energy store is the one that is the most readily available.

The largest store of energy is in the form of fat, which acts as the body's fuel reserve (see pages 18–21). Most fat is stored beneath the skin and around the body's internal organs.

FOOD GROUPS:
Getting All You Need

The substances in food that give us nourishment are called nutrients. They provide us with all the fuel we need to be active. Nutrients can be divided into two groups, according to how much of them we need.

The nutrients we need in large amounts are called **macronutrients** and those we need in smaller amounts are **micronutrients**. The main macronutrients are **carbohydrates**, **proteins**, and fats. They are contained in different quantities in all kinds of foods. Fats provide more energy than carbohydrates or proteins do. However, fats are not usually the best nutrients for sports and exercise (see pages 20–21).

▼ Food labels tell you everything you need to know about nutrients and other ingredients in food and drink. This makes it easy to compare different brands.

Macronutrients

The same weight of these three macronutrients provide different amounts of energy:

✔ Fats provide 256.5 calories per ounce (28 grams), or 9 calories (kcal) per gram.

✔ Carbohydrates provide 114 calories per ounce, or 4 calories per gram.

✔ Proteins provide 114 calories per ounce, or 4 calories per gram.

Fats are therefore the most concentrated provider of energy, giving more than twice as much energy as either carbohydrates or proteins.

The micronutrients are **vitamins** and **minerals**. We need only small amounts of these, and they do not provide us with energy. However, they help us stay healthy and prevent illness. They are important to everyone, including all athletes. Without micronutrients you would not perform at your best.

There are two other essential substances in food: water and **fiber**. Water is an essential part of blood, and so it helps carry nutrients around the body. Fiber is important because it aids the process of **digestion** by helping the body pass feces, or solid waste, easily.

A balanced diet

We can put foods into five main groups, based on what they contain. Like everyone else, athletes should eat more of the first two groups and less of the others.

✔ Bread, **cereal grains**, and potatoes, including rice and pasta: These starchy foods provide a lot of carbohydrates and fiber. They should make up about a third of the food you eat.

✔ Fruits and vegetables: Eat at least five portions every day. They give vitamins, fiber, and carbohydrates, and they should also make up about a third of your food.

✔ Milk and dairy products, including soy alternatives, such as soy milk for vegans: These are a good source of protein, vitamins, and **calcium**. We need moderate amounts of these foods.

✔ Meat, fish, and eggs, including beans, nuts, **lentils**, and other **pulses**: These foods contain a lot of protein and minerals. However, you should eat them in moderation.

✔ Fat and sugar, including cakes, cookies, chips, and soda: Fats and sugars have many calories and give lots of energy, but they have few nutrients. It is therefore not good to eat too much in this group.

CARBOHYDRATES:
The Energy Source

Carbohydrates are our most important source of energy. They provide fuel for the muscles as well as for the brain. The basic unit of carbohydrates is a sugar called **glucose**. Glucose forms what are called simple carbohydrates, which are found in fruit. When many **molecules** of glucose join together, they form complex carbohydrates. These are found in starchy foods, such as bread and potatoes.

▲ There is a wide range of high-carbohydrate foods.

WOW!

The brain needs about 5 ounces (about 600 calories) of glucose a day to function properly. The brain relies on the bloodstream to deliver a constant supply.

Simple carbohydrates = sugars
There are five different common sugars:

✔ Glucose, found in fruits and honey

✔ Fructose, in fruits, vegetables, and honey

✔ Lactose and galactose, in milk and dairy products

✔ Sucrose, in sugarcane and sugar beet (making table sugar)

✔ Maltose, in beer and malted foods (like some breakfast cereals).

Complex carbohydrates = starches
Starchy carbohydrates are found in bread, potatoes, pasta, rice, corn, **oats**, breakfast cereals, noodles, and **millet.** This is a group that should make up about a third of our diet.

FUEL IN THE BLOOD

The blood carries glucose from carbohydrates to all parts of our body, including our muscles. Extra glucose is stored in the liver and muscles in the form of glycogen, which can quickly be turned back into glucose when needed. This is how athletes get extra energy. When the level of sugar in the blood is low and muscles need more glucose, the liver turns glycogen back into glucose. This is why it is important for athletes to have high stores of glycogen before they take part in their sport.

People used to believe that simple carbohydrates (sugars) provided quick energy, while starches worked more slowly. However it is not as simple as that. Eating some starchy foods, such as bread and potatoes, also causes a quick rise in blood sugar level.

What do different foods contain?

3.5-oz (100-g) portion	carbo-hydrate (g)	protein (g)	fat (g)	fiber (g)	calories (kcal)
cornflakes	89.6	7.9	0.7	0.9	376
honey	82.4	0.3	0	0.2	304
brown rice	81.3	6.7	2.8	1.9	357
spaghetti	74.0	12.0	1.8	2.9	342
whole-grain bread	31.8	6.8	2.6	4.5	171
baked potato	31.0	3.9	0.2	2.7	136
banana	23.0	1.2	0.3	1.1	95
baked beans	15.1	4.8	0.6	3.5	81
apple	11.8	0.4	0.1	1.8	47
carrot	10.1	1.0	0.2	3.0	43
orange juice	8.8	0.5	0.1	0.1	36

SOCCER AND A HEALTHY DIET: EAT WELL TO PLAY WELL

On match days fat and protein intake should be restricted and an easily digested pre-match meal eaten about three hours before kick-off—with a "top-up" high-protein snack consumed 90 minutes later.[. . .] A baked potato, pasta or rice with a low-fat sauce, breakfast cereal with low-fat milk, or banana sandwiches are all foods that are not too bulky and are easily digested. For a high-carbohydrate snack try toast (or muffins) with jam or honey, or sweetened cereal. Drink orange juice with the meal and the snack.

From U.S. National Soccer Team Players Association

GLYCEMIC INDEX

Scientists have figured out what effect different foods have on blood-sugar levels. The **glycemic index** (GI) gives a number to each food, showing how fast it affects sugar levels in your blood. High-GI foods, which raise your blood-sugar level fast, have scores over 60. Moderate scores are 40 to 60. Low-GI foods have a score below 40. Athletes generally select low-GI foods before exercise and high-GI foods during and after exercise.

GI scores of some foods

food	portion size	GI rating
white rice	6.3 oz	87
baked potato	6.3 oz, medium	85
cornflakes	1 oz, small bowl	84
watermelon	7 oz, one slice	72
white bread	1.3 oz, large slice	70
granola	1.8 oz, small bowl	56
sweetcorn	3 oz	55
banana	3.5 oz	55
baked beans	7.2 oz, small can	48
macaroni	8.1 oz	45
pear	5.6 oz	38
fruit yogurt	5.3 oz	33

Note that figures may vary depending on the exact food, its origin, and how it was produced. The figures are averages; GI ratings differ from person to person.

Endurance test

Swedish scientists tested athletes on diets that were low, moderate, or high in carbohydrates. They all had to ride exercise bikes at the same pedal speed for as long as they could without stopping.

✔ Low-carb cyclists did 60 minutes

✔ Moderate-carb cyclists did 115 minutes

✔ High-carb cyclists managed 170 minutes.

▶ A group of Tour de France cyclists tackles the hilly roads of the Pyrenees mountains.

TOUR DE FRANCE

The Tour de France bicycle race is extremely demanding. Top professional cyclists cover around 2,237 miles (3,600 kilometers) in 21 stages, spread out over three weeks. The toughest stages include steep climbs in the Alps and Pyrenees mountains.

Tour de France riders take in about 6,000 to 7,000 calories a day. That is almost three times as much as an ordinary adult. They try to get about 70 percent of their energy from carbohydrates and spread the rest between proteins and fats. At breakfast and dinner, before and after the race, most riders eat lots of potatoes, rice, pasta, bread, fruits, and vegetables. They get protein from eggs, meat, and yogurt and get fats from olive oil used for cooking and cheese.

▲ Lance Armstrong, wearing the yellow jersey of the race leader, wins a stage of the Tour de France in 2004.

Riders try to take in about 300 to 400 calories every hour when they are racing. They eat small sandwiches and energy bars, which they carry in a small bag. They supplement this with sports drinks. All the riders take their eating and drinking very seriously. They know that it could win or lose them a stage, or even the tour.

Modern ideas about nutrition and fitness helped Lance Armstrong win the 2005 Tour de France at an average speed of 26 miles per hour (41.7 kilometers per hour). This was much faster than Maurice Garin of France, who won the first ever Tour in 1903 at a speed of 16 mph (25.8 kph). In those days, cyclists were allowed several days' rest between stages.

13

PROTEIN:
The Essential Body Builder

Protein makes up part of every cell in your body. Proteins build, maintain, and repair cells, and they are particularly important for growing children.

Proteins are large molecules made up of smaller chemicals called **amino acids**. When we eat proteins, they are broken down by digestion into acids. There are twenty different amino acids. Many of them can be made in the body from other substances, but nine of them have to be supplied in the food we eat. These are called essential amino acids.

Our cells are constantly being replaced, so protein needs to be taken in all the time. If there are not enough of the other two macronutrients (carbohydrates and fats), protein is also used to meet energy demands. Like carbohydrates and fats, protein cannot be stored for later use. If the body has more protein than it needs, the extra is broken down and used for energy.

▲ Peanut butter is made by grinding roasted peanuts into a paste. It is high in protein.

▲ Snowboarders work their muscles hard and need to be very fit and strong.

Enzymes are made of protein. They speed up chemical reactions in the body, and without them the cells could not function properly. **Hormones**, which are usually also made of protein, act as chemical messengers and control many bodily processes. A good example is adrenaline, which prepares the body for action by making the heart pump faster and by speeding up breathing. This hormone and many others are particularly important for athletes. They send more blood and oxygen to the muscles, and so improve performance.

MUSCLE POWER

Protein is important for building muscle tissue. This does not mean that the more protein you take in, the bigger and stronger your muscles will be. It is exercising them that makes your muscles larger. However, most athletes put their muscles under great strain. Because of this, they often suffer small muscle injuries during training and competition. Usually these are small tears in the muscle tissue. Proteins help repair these tears.

Most people in industrialized countries eat more protein than they need. Even top athletes should get enough protein from a normal, balanced diet. Many experts believe that it is not necessary for them to eat extra protein. Young athletes should certainly stick to a normal, balanced diet.

HIGH-PROTEIN FOODS

Plants make their own proteins from nutrients in the soil and water. Animals take proteins in when they eat plants, and their muscles are especially rich in essential amino acids. That is why meat is a good source of protein for humans.

Fish, milk, other dairy foods, and eggs are good sources, too. Vegetarians should make sure that they get enough protein by eating pulses, such as lentils, garbanzo beans, and other beans. **Tofu** and other soy products, as well as nuts and seeds, are also good protein sources. It is particularly good to eat high-protein foods that are low in fat. In this table of different foods, you can see that amounts of fat vary enormously.

What do different foods contain?

3.5-oz (100-g) portion	protein (g)	carbo-hydrate (g)	fat (g)	fiber (g)	calories (kcal)
steak, grilled	29.0	0	8.0	0	188
peanuts	25.6	12.5	46.0	6.2	563
salmon, cooked	25.5	0	4.4	0	149
cheddar cheese	25.4	1.4	33.6	0	407
dried lentils	24.0	48.8	1.9	8.9	297
cashew nuts	20.5	18.8	50.9	3.2	611
egg	12.5	0	10.8	0	151
spaghetti	12.0	74.0	1.8	2.9	342
cornflakes	7.9	89.6	0.7	0.9	376
whole-grain bread	6.8	31.8	2.6	4.5	171
brown rice	6.7	81.3	2.8	1.9	357
baked beans	4.8	15.1	0.6	3.5	81
milk, skim	3.4	4.7	1.7	0	46

HIGH-PROTEIN VERSUS HIGH-CARB

Steak, eggs, and high-protein drinks have been shunned for years by sports nutritionists, who claim that a high-carb approach is the only way to enhance sports performance. But a study at the University of Illinois, published in the *Journal of Nutrition*, found athletes who consumed more protein (low-fat dairy food, lean meat, etc.) to be faster, stronger, and leaner. "There's an interactive effect when a protein-rich diet is combined with exercise," says Professor Donald Layman, who led the study. "The two work together to correct body composition; dieters lose more weight, and they lose fat, not muscle."

Copyright *Guardian Newspapers Limited*, October 15, 2005

STRENGTH AND POWER VS. ENDURANCE

High protein levels are essential for sports that require a great deal of strength and power as well as those that need great endurance. This is because both kinds of sports need high muscular fitness.

What is the difference between a "strength and power" sport and an "endurance" sport? Think of lifting weights. A person needs strength and power to lift a heavy weight and endurance to lift a weight many times. Examples of strength/power sports are track and field, wrestling, gymnastics, and football. Endurance sports are long-distance running, cycling, swimming, hockey, and soccer.

Be careful!

Most doctors and sports experts do not encourage young people to lift heavy weights or overdo strength/power or endurance sports. This is because their growing bodies may be more at risk of stresses and injuries. Always make sure that you are guided and helped by a qualified coach.

▼ Greco-Roman wrestlers use only their arms and upper bodies, not their legs, to grapple with their opponent. For Olympic competition, this power sport is divided into seven weight categories, from less than 121 pounds (55 kg) all the way up to 264 pounds (120 kg).

FATS:
Essential for a Balanced Diet

Fats make up the third macronutrient, and they are also an essential part of a balanced diet. Some people think that fats are bad for them because they are so high in calories, but we all need some fat in our diet, including **essential fatty acids**. Fat is needed both for energy and to help our bodies absorb important vitamins.

Some fats are much better than others for all of us, including athletes. Fatty acids contain atoms of the **elements** carbon, hydrogen, and oxygen. Those with many hydrogen atoms are called **saturated fats**, and they are often called "bad fats." This is because eating a lot of saturated fats increases a person's risk of developing heart disease.

Fats with fewer hydrogen atoms are called **unsaturated fats** and are generally liquid. They are "good fats" because of a reduced risk of heart disease. A fat with one unsaturated fatty acid is called monounsaturated, and good sources include olive oil and rapeseed oil (also called canola oil). Fats with more than one unsaturated fatty acid, such as sunflower and soy oil, are called polyunsaturated.

▲ Saturated fats are mostly solid at room temperature and include butter, hard cheese, such as cheddar, and fatty meat, such as bacon.

▲ The body stores fat in fat cells. These cells have been magnified over 500 times.

Omega-3 fatty acids are polyunsaturated fats found in oily fish. They are believed to help reduce the risk of heart disease. As you will see from the table on page 20, foods can contain different combinations of these fats.

BODY FAT IN SPORTS

Body fat is generally a disadvantage in sports. It makes athletes heavy and slows them down. Even when athletes are very heavy, a greater percentage of muscle is usually better than fat. People used to think that fat was an advantage in sports such as discus and hammer throwing, wrestling, and judo. In fact, muscle is still more of an advantage than fat.

What do different foods contain?

3.5-oz (100-g) portion	total fat (g)	saturated fat (g)	monoun-saturated fat (g)	polyun-saturated fat (g)	calories (kcal)
olive oil	91.0	13.0	71.0	7.0	820
butter	80.0	52.0	20.7	2.7	747
cashew nuts	50.9	10.1	29.4	9.1	611
peanuts	46.0	8.7	22.0	13.0	563
cheddar cheese	33.6	21.4	9.6	1.1	407
grilled bacon	26.8	9.8	11.5	3.7	337
avocado	19.3	2.5	12.0	2.6	190
lean ground beef	14.3	5.5	5.7	0.5	244
herring, cooked	12.4	2.8	5.1	2.9	216
egg	10.8	3.1	4.5	1.7	151

Fat choices

Different foods vary greatly in their levels of saturated fat. Of the top five in the list above, the percentages of saturates in the total fat are:

✔ Butter 65%

✔ Cheddar cheese 64%

✔ Cashew nuts 20%

✔ Peanuts 19%

✔ Olive oil 14%

Some other cheeses have less saturated fat than cheddar. Italian mozzarella cheese, for example, has a little over half the saturated fat content of cheddar. Many cooks choose to use olive oil rather than other fats, such as butter, for cooking because olive oil contains much less saturated fat.

EXCEPTIONAL SUMO

The ancient Japanese sport of sumo wrestling is the exception as far as body fat is concerned. This may be partly because of tradition, but fat does give a real advantage. This is because the object of the sport is to push the opponent out of the ring or make him touch the floor with any part of his body except the soles of his feet. Speed and agility can be important, but the heavier wrestler usually wins.

Top sumo wrestlers have strong muscles, but it is most important for them to have lots of fat around the belly and hips. This lowers their center of gravity and makes it much harder to push them off balance. They train to be heavy and may reach a weight of up to 584 pounds (265 kg). That is more than three times heavier than an average adult man.

▲ Asashoryu Akinori was the first Mongolian wrestler to reach the highest sumo rank. Here he performs a ceremony before a wrestling match.

CHUNKY *CHANKO*

Chanko, the traditional dish of sumo wrestlers, is a hearty stew with meat or seafood and vegetables. During sumo tournaments most wrestlers eat the chicken version, because they believe that chickens bring good luck. (Chickens walk on two legs, which is how the wrestlers want to remain.) Salt is also considered a good thing. Before a match, wrestlers usually scatter a handful of salt in the ring to guard against evil spirits and injuries.

Some typical *chanko* ingredients are chicken, potatoes, egg noodles, onions, carrots, leeks, radishes, mushrooms, cabbage, deep-fried tofu, soy sauce, sweet rice wine, and salt. Wrestlers eat large amounts to gain weight. The ingredients are not particularly fatty, but they contain a huge number of calories, so the body stores the excess as fat. Many wrestlers sleep for several hours after eating an enormous meal.

VITAMINS AND MINERALS:
A Little Goes a Long Way

Vitamins and minerals are called micronutrients because we need so little of them. Tiny quantities are enough, but they are still essential. Vitamins and minerals do not provide us with energy, but they help the body use food properly and so affect our energy levels.

Vitamins are chemical compounds that are found in plants, animals, some yeasts, and bacteria. There are at least thirteen vitamins. They are sometimes known by their chemical names and also by letter codes (thiamin and B1 are the same vitamin, for example). Vitamins are very important because they regulate the chemical reactions used by the body to convert food into energy. Vitamins B and C are soluble (dissolve) in water and the body cannot store them. We need a constant supply of these vitamins from our food.

Minerals are metals and other elements that are found naturally in the ground. We need traces of about fifteen minerals. The major minerals are calcium, phosphorus, potassium, sodium, magnesium, iron, and zinc. They are also essential because they help make bones, bodily fluids, and substances that help the body function properly.

◀ Citrus fruits, such as oranges, lemons, limes, and grapefruit, are a good source of vitamin C.

▲ Spinach is a good source of iron, vitamins A and C, and many other vitamins and minerals.

What do different foods contain?

3.5-oz (100-g) portion	vitamin B 1 (mg)	vitamin C (mg)	calcium (mg)	iron (mg)
apple	0.03	6.0	4	0.1
banana	0.05	9.1	6	0.3
baked beans	0.09	0	53	1.4
beef, ground	0.05	0	18	3.1
cabbage	0.15	49.0	52	0.7
cheddar cheese	0.03	0	720	0.3
cornflakes	1.00	0	15	6.7
milk	0.03	1.0	115	0.06
sardines, canned	0.04	0	550	2.9
spaghetti, boiled	0.01	0	7	0.5
white bread	0.21	0	110	1.6

These are tiny amounts of vitamins and minerals. One milligram (mg) is one thousandth of a gram.

Especially for athletes

These four substances are particularly useful in the following ways:

✔ Vitamin B 1 (thiamin) is found in vegetables, pulses, nuts, meat, and **whole grains**. It helps the body release energy from carbohydrates in food.

✔ Vitamin C, also called ascorbic acid, is found in fruits and vegetables. It helps build healthy blood vessels, bones, and gums. It also helps to produce collagen, a substance that holds tissues together.

✔ Calcium is found in most foods, and especially in milk and dairy products. It is essential for building strong bones and helps muscles work well.

✔ Iron is plentiful in meat, spinach, pulses, dried fruit, and sardines. It is essential for helping to form the different substances that carry oxygen in the blood and in muscle cells.

Eating a balanced diet is the best way to obtain enough of these vitamins.

VITAMIN AND MINERAL SUPPLEMENTS

Many athletes take extra vitamins and minerals in the form of pills. Some believe that these **supplements** improve both their health and their performance. There have been many studies to try to prove this one way or the other. Most studies have shown that supplements really only help athletes who are very low on a particular vitamin or mineral. If this is the case, the person should be seen by a doctor.

There is often a big difference between what people believe and real scientific evidence. Some of the studies quoted by the companies that sell supplements may not have been very thorough. Some top athletes may believe in certain substances because they think they have worked wonders for them. This may not really be the case.

Too much can sometimes be a bad thing. For example, too much vitamin A can cause nausea and even liver damage. Too much vitamin D can result in high blood pressure or kidney problems.

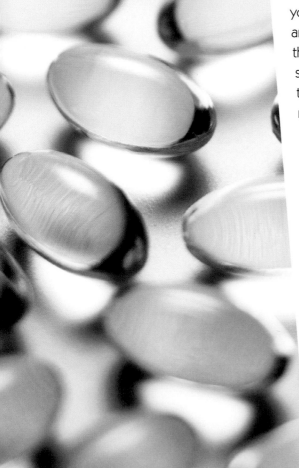

If you have a good, balanced diet, you will be getting all the minerals and vitamins you need—as well as all the nutrients. You will not need any supplements. These should never be taken without consulting a medical expert.

Some sports scientists recommend that adult athletes take extra magnesium or calcium, since both are important minerals for the function of muscles. However, unless the player has a deficiency in either mineral, the supplements will not make much of a difference. Some athletes believe that chromium pills can help them burn off fat.

◀ Fish-oil capsules contain omega-3 fatty acids (see page 19) and vitamin E.

Others believe chromium can help build extra muscle. Yet research has shown that the pills do not help. It has even been suggested that too much chromium can cause problems.

Leg cramps and muscle pain are very common in all sports because of the strain put on muscles. This sharp pain is called a "charley horse," which is thought to be a baseball term dating from the 1880s. It may have come from a player's name, or even the name of a groundskeeper's horse! Many athletes used to take salt pills, thinking that they helped against cramps and other muscle problems. Salt supplements can irritate the stomach and cause people to feel sick and even vomit.

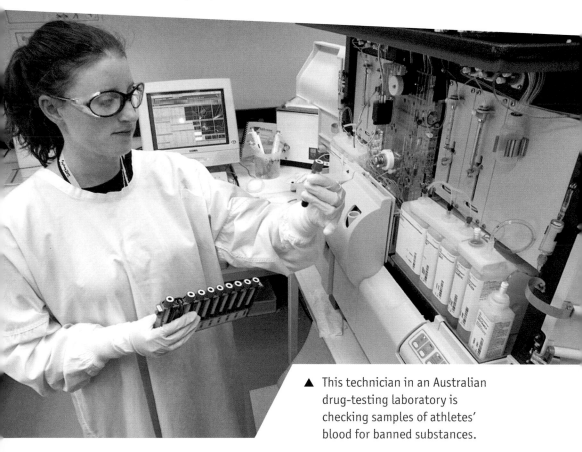

▲ This technician in an Australian drug-testing laboratory is checking samples of athletes' blood for banned substances.

BANNED SUBSTANCES

Sports ban the use of performance-enhancing drugs, such as steroids. There have been some cases in which athletes who have failed drug tests claim that the results were caused by legal dietary supplements bought in a pharmacy or health-food store. This is possible, but most sports authorities take a tough line. Top athletes need to be very careful about what they add to their diet.

FLUIDS:
Vital to Our Health

Did you know that you can survive much longer without food than without water? Water is vital to our health. It is an essential part of blood and so helps carry nutrients around the body. It is needed for the breakdown of energy. Water also makes up **urine**, which helps to take waste products from the body.

The reason we have to drink a lot is because we need to replace the water that our body uses all the time. In hot weather you need to drink more because the body loses so much through sweating. This is why drinking is so important to athletes. About three-quarters of the energy put into exercise is turned into heat. An athlete may produce 20 calories (kcal) of heat energy every minute, and this has to be removed from the body.

▼ This cyclist has been sweating a great deal during his race. He needs to drink a lot to replace lost fluids.

That is why sports involve so much sweat. Water from your body is carried to your skin as sweat, where it evaporates so that you lose heat. The harder you exercise, the hotter you get, and the more you sweat. The more you sweat, the more you need to drink to replace the water.

During exercise an average athlete might use up about 2 pints (1 liter) of fluid. A serious marathon runner might lose twice as much as that on a hot day. The amounts vary according to the athlete's size, weight, and fitness.

HOW MUCH WATER?

Most people need about six to eight glasses, or 2.5 pints (1.2 liters), of fluid a day, plus however much they lose during exercise. The most important thing is to make sure that you are well **hydrated** before exercise. This means drinking plenty of fluid before the event. Then add an extra 5 fluid ounces (150 ml) or more just before you start.

During exercise try to drink small amounts frequently—about 5 fluid ounces (150 mL) every fifteen minutes or so. After exercise, drink plenty immediately and continue drinking until you are no longer thirsty.

CHANGING SPORTS HABITS

Individual sports coaches often have their own beliefs and ways of doing things as far as nutrition is concerned. Professional coaches may insist on major changes in eating and drinking habits among the players on their teams. In recent years some soccer coaches, for example, have altered their players' dinner menus completely. Some have reduced the players' intake of red meat, dairy products, fried food, and sugar, replacing them with more vegetables, fish, chicken and plenty of water. To control player's levels of hydration, they use urine charts (see below) to check that they are drinking enough water.

Urine charts

Urine charts are small, laminated cards with eight color strips on them. The idea is for athletes to compare the color of their urine with the chart.

✔ If it is similar to numbers 1–3 (shades of very pale yellow), the player is fine.

✔ The yellow color of numbers 4 and 5 mean that the player is dehydrated.

✔ Numbers 6–8 (dark yellow to light brown) show severe dehydration.

DEHYDRATION

Dehydration is a major problem for any athlete. If you are dehydrated, you will suddenly feel weak and dizzy. You may also suffer from cramping and feel a headache coming on. It is essential to cool down and drink as quickly as possible.

Dehydration is not only a problem in warm climates. It can happen when you are skiing or snowboarding, too. The dry, cold air of the mountains also has an effect. As you glide down the mountain, you are losing water through your breath as well as your sweat. However, the cold reduces your sensation of thirst, which makes the problem worse. Skiing instructors encourage everyone to drink a lot of water.

In a scientific study, runners ran a long-distance race twice under the same conditions on different occasions. The first time they drank their usual amount, but on the other occasion they were purposely slightly dehydrated. Their times suffered by 7 percent—more than two minutes over 6.2 miles (10,000 meters).

▼ A soccer player celebrates victory with a sports drink.

ALCOHOL AND DEHYDRATION

Alcoholic drinks make people want to urinate more. This means that alcohol can quickly cause dehydration. It also reduces coordination and decreases reaction time. Drinking alcohol can also lead to a wide range of health problems, and so young people should avoid it.

SPORTS DRINKS

You have probably seen sports drinks advertised. You may also have noticed that sports stars usually have their own individual drinks or use a special sports drink. Some people may think that this is all just advertising and an attempt to sell more products, but sports drinks really do work.

They contain carbohydrates (usually in the form of glucose, which is a type of sugar) to provide energy. They also contain **electrolytes**, which help control fluid balance in the body. Sports drinks are absorbed into the body faster than water. They also make you want to drink more. Some sports drinks have added vitamins as well as flavorings, colors, and additives. Drinking water is still the best way to rehydrate, but sports drinks can also help and provide extra energy.

What's the difference?

There are three different kinds of sports drinks:

✔ *Isotonic drinks* contain about the same concentration of carbohydrates and electrolytes as the body's own fluids (4–8 grams of carbohydrate per 100 milliliters of fluid).

✔ *Hypotonic drinks* contain a lower concentration (less than 4 g/100 ml); these are absorbed faster than water but do not contribute much energy.

✔ *Hypertonic drinks* have a higher concentration (more than 8 g/100 ml); these are absorbed more slowly than water.

OVERHYDRATION

Some athletes who compete in endurance events, such as triathlons, can suffer from overhydration. This happens when they take in lots of water, but not enough electrolytes to replace the ones lost. Some signs of overhydration include confusion, disorientation, and nausea. Sport drinks help you avoid having too much water in your system and not enough of the natural salts your body needs.

TAKING CARE OF YOUR BODY:
It's the Only One You Have

Our bodies are not all the same shape, but we can all take part in sports. No matter what your shape, if you are healthy, you can enjoy exercise and sports. Exercise will then get you fit and keep you feeling well!

Scientists divide people into three basic body shapes, though most of us combine some of these characteristics. The three types are:

- Ectomorph: thin and delicate
- Mesomorph: compact and muscular
- Endomorph: round, with more body fat.

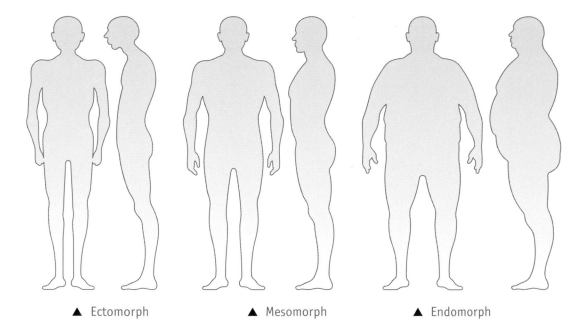

▲ Ectomorph   ▲ Mesomorph   ▲ Endomorph

Most successful athletes are in the medium mesomorph range. That is because they have a good combination of the two main bodily elements: lean body tissue (including muscle) and body fat. Muscles are obviously useful in any sport, but fat seldom helps performance.

THE BODY MASS INDEX

Scientists have figured out ways to help people check that they are the right weight. The best-known way is the Body Mass Index (BMI). This compares a person's weight to his or her height. There is no ideal weight, but there is a healthy range. The BMI was developed in 1846 by a Belgian mathematician and astronomer, Adolphe Quetelet (1796–1874). It is still sometimes called the Quetelet Index.

The BMI is simply a guide, and it is intended for healthy adults. It is not suitable for younger people who are still growing and whose bodies are still developing.

An adult person's BMI is calculated by dividing his or her weight (in pounds) by the square of his or her height (in inches) and multiplying this by 703. This results in a figure that can be compared with this scale:

✔ less than 17.5 = underweight

✔ 17.5–24.9 = normal range

✔ 25–29.9 = overweight

✔ 30+ = obese

A person who is 5 feet, 3 inches (1.6 meters) tall and weighs 120 pounds (54 kilograms) has a BMI of 21.3. This falls within the normal range. There are many calculators on the Internet that you can use to calculate your BMI.

Athletes with very well-developed muscles often find that they fall into the overweight category on BMI and other tests. This can be misleading, because they probably have a healthy body shape with very little fat.

Adult athletes can undergo other tests to check their body composition and especially their fat distribution. This includes using calipers, which are like a large pair of tweezers, to measure the layer of fat on the body's surface. They do this to make sure their body is allowing them to perform at their best.

APPLES AND PEARS

People who have too much weight around their middle are said to have an "apple" shape. They have excess fat stored in the stomach area, and this may increase their risk of developing heart disease and diabetes. If their weight is mainly around the hips and bottom, they have what is called a "pear" shape. This is generally healthier than the apple shape.

FLUCTUATING WEIGHT

A person's weight does not stay the same all the time. Small losses or gains are perfectly normal. A healthy adult might fluctuate by up to 4.4 pounds (2 kilograms) a day.

If you think you are overweight, do not just go on a weight-loss diet. You should only do this under the supervision of a qualified health specialist. It is more important to stick to a balanced diet. At the same time, it is good to cut down on sweet foods, such as cakes and soda, as well as fatty foods, such as burgers and French fries.

SHORT, LIGHT, AND STRONG

Gymnastics is one of the oldest sports in the world. It was popular in ancient Greece, where it was used as a way to train young men to be fit for battle. The modern form of the sport began in the early 1800s in Sweden, and it soon spread to Germany and other countries.

WOW!

In the first modern Olympic Games, which took place in Athens in 1896, there were eight men's events. One of these was rope-climbing. This was judged on the time it took to get to the top.

Top gymnasts are generally short and light. Yet they have to be amazingly strong and have great explosive power. They also need both balance and flexibility.

Top gymnasts tend to be young compared to other athletes. Romanian gymnast Nadia Comaneci was just fourteen years old when she won three Olympic gold medals in 1976. Her achievements included the first ever perfect score of ten in an Olympic gymnastic event—and she scored seven of them! At the 2004 Olympics in Athens, Greece, the women's all-around winner was the U.S. gymnast Carly Patterson, who was sixteen years old and 4 feet, 9 inches (1.45 meters) tall.

Gymnasts need to be very fit and healthy so that they can put in long hours of practice. Patterson, for example, trained for up to 35 hours every week. That is an average of seven hours a day, five days a week!

Young people who take up gymnastics become very aware of the way their body looks. This is because it is an aesthetic sport, which means that the beauty of their movements is important. Their performance is scored by a team of judges who watch the gymnasts very carefully.

BODY IMAGE

Many young female gymnasts work hard to be thin. There is a danger that they might not eat enough nutritious food. This can lead to problems and eating disorders (see page 45). Research at U.S. universities shows that many female gymnasts want to lose weight and be thinner. Yet many young male gymnasts want to build up their muscles and gain weight.

▲ Chinese gymnast Li Ya shows amazing elegance and athleticism on the balance beam. The wooden beam is just 3.9 inches (10 cm) wide and stands 3.9 feet (1.2 m) off the floor.

VEGETARIAN ATHLETES

Vegetarians are people who do not eat meat. Some eat fish or seafood, and many are happy to eat a few animal products, such as milk, cheese, and eggs. Vegans do not eat any foods of animal origin, including all dairy products and honey (which is made by bees).

Nutritionists agree that a vegetarian diet can be perfectly healthy. Meat contains a lot of protein, so vegetarians and vegans have to make sure they get plenty of protein from other sources. They must also make sure they get enough vitamins, especially B 12, and minerals such as iron, zinc, and calcium.

◀ Beans, lentils, and peas are a good source of protein and iron.

Good foods for vegetarians		
	sources	**more information**
protein	beans, peas, and lentils; nuts and seeds; soy products; **textured vegetable protein**; milk, cheese, and yogurt; eggs	
vitamin B 12	soy products; fortified breakfast cereals; dairy products; eggs	some cereals and foods are fortified with B 12
iron	green leafy vegetables; dried fruit; pulses and seeds; fortified breakfast cereals	orange juice should be drunk with iron-rich foods (vitamin C helps the body absorb iron)
zinc	whole-grain bread; pulses, nuts and seeds; eggs	
calcium	spinach and broccoli; seeds and nuts; fortified soy products; dairy products	

EDWIN MOSES

U.S. athlete Ed Moses dominated one of the world's toughest sports for ten years. As a vegetarian, he showed that you can be super-fit and strong without eating meat. Moses burst onto the world scene when he won the gold medal in the 400-meter hurdles at the 1976 Olympics in Montreal, Canada. He won a second gold eight years later, in Los Angeles.

Moses improved the world record in his event four times. Between September 1977 and June 1987, he won 122 races, including 107 400-meter hurdles finals in a row! The wins included two World Championship golds and three World Cup titles. At the 1988 Olympics in Seoul, South Korea, Moses won a bronze medal. This was the final race of his career.

WOW!

In a study in 1994, vegetarian and meat-eating runners were checked after running 621 miles (1,000 kilometers) over twenty days. They were given foods that had the same nutrients and total energy. The results showed that the diets did not affect their performance.

▲ Ed Moses is shown in full flight.

TRAINING AND COMPETING:
Eating to Be Fast

For young athletes and those who enjoy their sport on a social level, what they eat should stay the same most of the time. Even with a competition coming up, they should stick to their normal routine. This involves making sure that they eat a variety of foods every day and drink plenty of fluids so that they are well hydrated.

Top athletes may change their diet slightly when important competitions come up. But they always take training days seriously and use the same eating habits as they will during a big event. That way, there are no big surprises on competition day.

▶ Runners train for a long-distance event.

LEADING UP TO A LONG RACE

Long-distance runners try to make sure that they are at their peak of health and fitness for their race. This includes having their energy levels at their highest. One of the most grueling races is the marathon, which covers a distance of 26 miles and 385 yards (42.2 kilometers).

For at least a week before the race, marathon runners eat plenty of foods that are rich in carbohydrates. They do this to fill up their glycogen stores (see page 7) so that it will be as if they have a full tank of fuel on the big day. During this week runners eat lots of bread, rice, pasta, cereals, potatoes, fruits, and vegetables.

The day before the big race, runners eat as much carbohydrates as they can. However, they avoid whole-grain foods, because these take a long time to digest. They also avoid any foods that they are not totally used to, because they want to avoid an upset stomach at all costs. Meals are supplemented with high-carbohydrate snacks such as cereal bars.

ON THE DAY

Marathon runners have a meal (normally breakfast) two or three hours before the race. It is not good to run on an empty stomach. They choose foods that are high in carbohydrates, such as cereal, toast and jam, or pancakes. They drink a glass of fruit juice or a sports drink.

Again, there should be nothing new in the meal: top athletes practice their pre-race eating routine many times in training. Pre-race nerves also play a part and make it difficult to eat too much.

During the race, runners grab a drink at the water stations. To keep hydrated, they drink little and often. In the major marathon races, there are usually drink stations every mile (1.6 kilometers). Runners grab a plastic bottle, drink it on the run, and then discard it at the side of the road.

Women's marathon

✔ In April 2003 British athlete Paula Radcliffe broke her own marathon world record by nearly two minutes, setting a new time of 2 hours, 15 minutes, and 25 seconds (2:15:25).

✔ Women have improved their long-distance times dramatically in recent years. The Olympic marathon was only introduced for women in 1984. The men's record of 2:04:55 was set in 2003 by Paul Tergat of Kenya. This is nearly eleven minutes faster than the women's record. Back in 1958 the fastest man was just eight seconds quicker than the current women's record.

▲ High-altitude training can help athletes. Their bodies must work harder due to the lack of oxygen in the air.

FIRST OLYMPIC WINNER

U.S. athlete Joan Benoit was born in Cape Elizabeth, Maine, in 1957. As a teenager her favorite sport was skiing, but after breaking a leg on the slopes, she took up running as part of her recovery. In 1979 she won the women's race at the Boston Marathon, but unfortunately she had to have knee surgery just seventeen days before the first-ever Olympic woman's marathon. This took place in Los Angeles in 1984. Nevertheless, Benoit was at the start line, and she dominated the race. She left the others behind and won in a time of 2 hours, 24 minutes, and 52 seconds—more than a minute ahead of her rivals. She became a legend in women's running.

You have to be at least eighteen to run in a city marathon, such as those held in Boston or New York. Many cities organize half-marathons (13.1 miles, or 21.1 km), also for people eighteen years and over. There are also much shorter fun runs (around 1 mile) for younger athletes, in which children are welcome. There is a fourteen- to nineteen-year age group for the Boston half-marathon. The Boston Athletic Association also holds Mayor's Cup races over 1.1 miles (1.8 kilometers) in the city's Franklin Park, with divisions for boys and girls in different age groups.

If you are interested in running, as a serious sport or just for fun, get in touch with your school team or local running club. An expert will make sure that you have fun learning to run the right distance at the right pace for your age and fitness.

AFTER THE EVENT

After competition, whether a long run or a game of tennis, the first aim is to build up energy again and make up for fluid losses. What you eat depends on whether you have finished for the day or have another event in a few hours. In any case, drinking is important, along with eating carbohydrate-rich foods, such as pasta or a baked potato. Rich or fatty foods should always be avoided.

▶ Tennis players have a short break at every changeover (after every two games). Here Venus Williams takes a drink of water.

THE FASTEST PEOPLE ON EARTH

Who would you call the ultimate athletes? There are many candidates. Many people think the most amazing athletes are those who combine many events. Male and female triathletes swim, cycle, and run very long distances. Male decathletes compete in ten athletic events and female heptathletes do seven.

At every Olympic Games and World Championship, the most popular spectator event is the 100-meter sprint. The winner of the men's event is often called the fastest human on earth. The current world record is 9.77 seconds, which means an average speed of 22.9 miles per hour (mph). That is nearly 37 kilometers per hour (kph). Back in 1896 the world's fastest sprinter managed 19 mph (30 kph). In the women's event, sprinters have improved by 2.3 seconds (nearly 4 mph, or 6.2 kph). How did sprinters gain that extra speed?

▼ Sprinters blast off their starting blocks at the 2004 Olympics in Athens, Greece.

Getting faster!

Some of the men's 100-m sprint world record holders, 1896–2005		Some of the women's 100-m sprint world record holders, 1922–2005	
12.0 Thomas Burke (U.S.A.)	1896	12.8 Mary Lines (GB)	1922
11.0 Frank Jarvis (U.S.A.)	1900	12.0 Betty Robinson (U.S.A.)	1928
10.4 Charles Paddock (U.S.A.)	1921	11.5 Helen Stephens (U.S.A.)	1936
10.2 Jesse Owens (U.S.A.)	1936	11.0 Wyomia Tyus (U.S.A.)	1968
10.0 Armin Hary (West Germany)	1960	10.9 Renate Stecher (East Germany)	1973
9.90 Leroy Burrell (U.S.A.)	1991	10.88 Marlies Oelsner (East Germany)	1977
9.86 Carl Lewis (U.S.A.)	1991	10.87 Lyudmila Kondratyeva (USSR)	1980
9.84 Donovan Bailey (Canada)	1996	10.81 Marlies Göhr (East Germany)	1983
9.79 Maurice Greene (U.S.A.)	1999	10.79 Evelyn Ashford (U.S.A.)	1983
9.77 Asafa Powell (Jamaica)	2005	10.49 Florence Griffith-Joyner (U.S.A.)	1988

Since 1988 five different male sprinters have improved the men's 100-meter world record. During that time the women's record holder remained the same: Florence Griffith-Joyner (known as "Flo-Jo"), who died in 1998. She won three sprint gold medals at the 1988 Olympics, as well as one silver medal. She once said, "I trained a lot harder for the '88 Olympics. There is no substitute for hard work—I have the medals to prove it."

HOW TO GAIN SPEED

The main way to get faster is by using more modern training techniques. An important part of these is nutrition. Nutrition is the science of what you eat and how it affects your body. Getting their diet right helps sprinters train harder and longer. In turn, intense training helps them improve their fitness and technique so that they get faster.

Like all other athletes, sprinters choose a high-carbohydrate diet. This is especially useful for the quick, fast-burn energy they need. They also need great muscular power, which they build through weight-training. Sprinters need to be strong and muscular, but at the same time they require low body-fat levels. Sprinters therefore look for low-fat foods.

Overall, a sprinter might take in up to three times as much energy (in calories) as an ordinary person. This might include a slightly higher proportion of carbohydrates, roughly the same proportion of protein, and a smaller percentage of fat.

SPRINTERS ON COMPETITION DAY

Sprinters have to be very careful about their diet on race days. Though each race lasts only seconds, they may have to run several heats and a final in one day. There is also a lot of waiting around. They normally start the day with a carbohydrate-based breakfast. Then they eat easily digested snacks and drink lots of fluids during the day. Their aim is to not feel hungry, but at the same time not to have an uncomfortably full stomach.

Even faster?

✔ A mathematician might say that 200-meter runners are fastest! The world record is 19.32 seconds, set by Michael Johnson (U.S.A.) in 1996. This works out to an average speed of 23.2 mph (37.3 kph). That average is faster than the 100-meter record. That's because a 200-meter runner starts the second 100 meters of the race at full speed and does not have to accelerate twice.

✔ This is not the case with the women's records. Both were set by Florence Griffith-Joyner in 1988. Her 10.49 seconds for the 100-meter race (21.3 mph, or 34.3 kph) is faster than her 21.34 seconds for the 200 meters (20.9 mph, or 33.7 kph).

SCIENTISTS AND SPECIALISTS

Professional athletes rely on experts to help them make the right food choices for their very important diet. This is only possible because so much study and research have gone into what different foods contain and how they affect the human body. This research is carried out by food scientists and nutritionists.

▶ Food scientists carry out tests in a laboratory.

Dietitians are specially trained and qualified experts who help people with all aspects of nutrition and diet. Some dietitians specialize in sports, and they work with individual athletes, sports teams, and qualified coaches. They give advice on the best diet for particular sports and events. They may have a degree or diploma in sport dietetics.

Many top professional athletes have their own dietitian. They get advice on special diets for training and competition. Their health and performance are checked regularly to see that their personal nutrition program is correct. Professional sports teams also have their own diet experts to take care of individual players.

▲ A specialist fitness coach guides players of the French national soccer team as they warm up for a training session.

CARBO STRATEGY

Consuming carbohydrates during exercise is an important strategy for endurance events like marathons. When an athlete eats is often an issue of opportunity provided by the sport (for example, at aid stations or at scheduled breaks), rather than a scientific ideal. The main advice is to eat carbohydrates early in exercise, rather than waiting till an athlete feels tired and fatigued. Early intake is also important in the recovery phase (after the exercise). An immediate intake of carbohydrates will ensure athletes replace glycogen in their muscles. This is especially important when the next bout of training or competition is in less than 8–12 hours.

HEALTH PROBLEMS:
Why a Good Diet Is So Important

Athletes on a good diet are less likely to have health problems than those who are not. Sensible nutrition can help athletes avoid illness and injury.

Food is important to all of us in terms of our general health. Proteins have a special role to play because they help repair damaged cells. Minerals and vitamins are also essential to health. Some athletes take extra vitamins, such as vitamin C to fight colds, in the belief that they keep them healthy.

What causes a side ache?

✔ Have you ever suffered from a pain in your side when running? Most people have. This annoying pain can often force runners to stop altogether. Some people think that this pain is caused by eating or drinking too much just before setting out. This may be a factor.

✔ Scientific research has found a different cause for this pain, which sports scientists call ETAP (exercise-related transient abdominal pain). They believe that the pain is caused by a spasm or cramp in the abdominal muscle.

✔ Soccer players, football players, swimmers, and basketball players can also suffer from it. Fit athletes suffer less, which may be because they have a better breathing technique. Probably the best tips for avoiding this pain are to get fit and to remember to breathe properly!

PROBLEMS WITH WEIGHT

Most athletes feel that they perform best at a certain weight. In some sports there are weight limits, which increase the pressure on athletes to watch their weight.

Many young people would like to be slimmer than they are. They might even be tempted to eat little and exercise a lot to try to get thinner. This is not a good idea.

If you are interested in long-distance sports, such as running or cycling, or aesthetic sports, such as gymnastics, figure skating, or diving, you might think it is important to be thin. However, the most important thing is to eat enough nourishing food to stay fit and healthy. Never try to lose weight drastically. This can lead to the development of an eating disorder, such as anorexia, which is very dangerous.

If you feel that you might have an eating or weight problem, or if you are just worried about your diet, it is important to ask for help. Speak at once to a parent, teacher, or another adult whom you trust, and be honest with yourself and them. Disordered eating will not make you a better athlete and will certainly give you many other problems.

▲ Boxer Laila Ali poses during an official weigh-in in December 2005. She is the daughter of boxing legend Muhammad Ali.

PREVENTING AND HEALING INJURIES

The fitter an athlete is, the less likely he or she is to get injured. We also know that good nutrition is an important part of general fitness. Many sports injuries are caused or made worse by tiredness. Surveys of both professional and vacationing skiers, for example, show that they fall and hurt themselves more toward the end of a day on the slopes. This is because tiredness makes their brain less alert and their muscles less responsive.

▼ An injured soccer player is put on a stretcher and carried from the field.

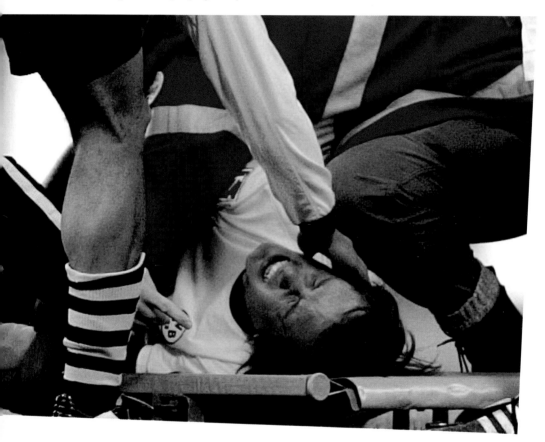

Proteins, vitamins, and minerals (especially iron, zinc, and calcium) all play an important part in the healing process when a athlete is injured. Professional athletes may find that they need to reduce their energy intake when they are injured. This is because they cannot burn off as many calories when they are not training. This will not affect young athletes, who should always continue with their normal diet.

Full-time athletes can use time off caused by injury to plan for the future. They may look at their diet plan and decide how they might change things when they get back to full training.

▼ Fruit is the perfect food to boost an athlete's energy.

Your balanced diet

Adult professional athletes may have special requirements for their particular activity. Some of them may take dietary supplements or eat an unusual mix of foods. You have read about some of these in this book. Remember that a growing young person's diet should always be varied and balanced. Your normal, healthy diet will give you all the energy you need for your chosen sport.

SPORTS AND FOOD FOR FUN

Sports are fun. They can help make you healthy and happy, and nutrition is an essential part of that. Though it is one of our most important basic needs, food can be fun, too. You can enjoy your favorite meals and have special treats that form part of a healthy, balanced diet.

47

IDEAS FOR HEALTHY EATING

Here are some ideas to help you enjoy healthy food along with your sports. Forget about dieting or giving up things you love, but try to stick to a few rules. Eat a lot of fruits and vegetables. Make sure there is variety in your diet and avoid too many pre-prepared meals.

GRAB A SANDWICH!

Make a healthy, filling sandwich with thick slices of the following delicious breads:

- Whole-wheat
- Rye
- Sourdough
- Sunflower-seed
- Multigrain
- Three-seed
- Ciabatta
- Barley
- Pita.

SOME SUGGESTED SANDWICH FILLINGS

- Hummus with lettuce and chopped peppers or grated carrot
- Peanut butter with sliced banana
- Tuna with watercress
- Tomatoes, mozzarella, and salad leaves
- Chopped chicken breast with arugula and sweet corn
- Guacamole (avocado with lemon juice and tomato)
- Hard-boiled egg with reduced-fat mayonnaise
- Cheese, sliced apple, and lettuce
- Marinated tofu with shredded carrots.

▲ Low-fat natural yogurt with strawberries is a great idea when you are in a hurry.

ON THE RUN

Here are some ideas for when you are in a hurry and need to grab something fast:

- Fresh fruit (apple, banana, pear, grapes, plum, peach, etc.)
- Low-fat fruit yogurt
- Fruit and cereal bar
- Rice cakes and crackers
- Whole-wheat rolls, pita bread, muffins, potato cakes, bagels filled with sliced banana, cottage cheese, peanut butter, olive spread
- Breakfast cereal or granola with skim milk
- Yogurt drinks
- Fruit juice.

A FEW MORE SUBSTANTIAL MEALS

- Baked potato filled with cottage cheese
- Mixed bean stew (with garbanzo, black, and kidney beans)
- Mixed vegetable stew (with zucchini, eggplant, tomatoes, and onions)
- Pasta with different sauces (such as tomato, mushroom, broccoli, and peppers; or leeks, spinach, and asparagus, with a little grated cheese)
- Vegetable stir-fries with tofu or cashew nuts
- Chicken or beef stir-fries
- Grilled whitefish with potatoes and steamed vegetables.

▼ Pasta is fun and easy to cook.

RECIPES

STIR-FRIED CHICKEN WITH BEAN SPROUTS AND NOODLES

This meal is quick to make. It also combines a good source of protein with vitamins A, B, and C, as well as folic acid and iron. A round, shallow pan, called a wok, allows you to use very little oil. If you do not have one, use a large nonstick frying pan. For a vegetarian stir-fry, add a handful of cashew nuts or chopped, smoked tofu instead of chicken. When stir-frying, you have to stir the chicken and vegetables all the time.

Ingredients:
$1/2$ pound boneless chicken breast, thinly sliced
2 tablespoons sunflower oil
2 cups Chinese noodles
2 cups bean sprouts
2 cups snow peas, broken in half
1 carrot, finely sliced
2 green onions, roughly chopped
$1/2$ inch root ginger, peeled and grated (optional)
3 oyster or other mushrooms, thinly sliced
1 tablespoon dark soy sauce
1 tablespoon sesame seeds
1 clove garlic, crushed (optional)
juice of 1 orange
1 tablespoon parsley, chopped

Method:
Cook the noodles in boiling water for 3–4 minutes, according to package instructions, and drain. Set them aside. Heat 1 tablespoon of oil in a wok, add the garlic and ginger, and cook for 10 seconds. Add the chicken and stir-fry over high heat for 2 minutes, until the meat is cooked through. Stir in the snow peas and carrot and fry for 2 minutes. Push to the side of the pan. Add the mushrooms and stir-fry for a further 2 minutes. Put this mixture into a bowl. Heat the rest of the oil in the same wok and add the bean sprouts and onion. Stir-fry for 1–2 minutes. Season with soy sauce. Return the chicken and vegetable mixture to the wok and stir in the orange juice and parsley. Reheat and mix well with the noodles. Cook for 2 minutes, until hot. Scatter with sesame seeds and serve at once.

▲ Vegetarian stir-fry can use tofu instead of chicken.

BERRY DELIGHT

Ingredients:

5 oz low-fat natural yogurt

¼ to ½ cup berries
(blueberries, raspberries,
strawberries)

1 teaspoon honey

1 tablespoon pumpkin and
sesame seeds

Method:

To toast the seeds, first heat a heavy-based frying pan until hot. Put the seeds in and stir over high heat, for about 1 minute. Leave to cool. Put the yogurt in a bowl and stir in the berries. Sprinkle with seeds and enjoy!

▲ Berry delight is a delicious snack.

GLOSSARY

amino acid substance that occurs naturally in the body and forms proteins

balanced diet diet with the right amounts of different kinds of foods

calcium mineral that helps build strong bones

calorie unit of energy

carbohydrate starch and sugar, found in food, that is converted to glucose when it is digested. The glucose is used for energy.

cell smallest microscopic part of a living thing

cereal grain seed from cereal plants, such as corn, wheat, or rice

diet kinds of food that a person usually eats

dietitian qualified expert who helps people with their diet and nutrition

digestion breaking down of food in the body

electrolyte mineral salt (such as sodium, potassium, and magnesium) that controls the balance of fluids in the body

element chemical substance that cannot be broken down into a simpler substance

enzyme substance that speeds up chemical reactions in the body

essential fatty acid type of acid found in fat that the body needs

fiber substance in plants that cannot be digested, but that helps people to digest food

glucose simple form of sugar found in many carbohydrates

glycemic index (or **GI**) system of numbers that shows how fast individual foods affect blood sugar after they have been eaten

glycogen substance stored in the muscles that changes to glucose and gives energy

hormone natural substance that regulates bodily processes

hydrated having enough water in the body

kilocalorie (kcal) unit of energy (equal to 1,000 calories, or 4.18 kilojoules)

kilojoule (kJ) unit of energy (equal to 1,000 joules, or 0.24 kilocalories)

lentil seed of a plant of the pea family

macronutrients substances in food (nutrients) that we need in large amounts, such as carbohydrates, proteins, and fats

micronutrients substances in food (nutrients) that we need in small amounts, such as vitamins and minerals

millet cereal plant that is grown for its grain

mineral chemical substance that occurs naturally in the soil and in foods. We need certain minerals in small quantities to be healthy.

molecule simple unit of a chemical substance

oat cereal plant that is grown for its grain

omega-3 fatty acid type of unsaturated fat mainly found in oily fish

organ part inside the body that has a special job to do

protein natural substance made up of amino acids that is needed for strength and growth

pulse seed of plants such as peas, beans, and lentils

saturated fat fat found in meat and animal products

supplement substance added to a person's diet, usually in the form of pills

textured vegetable protein defatted soy flour that has been processed and flavored so that it resembles meat

tissue body material made up of cells

tofu vegetarian food made from soy milk

unsaturated fat fat that has few hydrogen atoms

urine fluid made up of waste products that is stored in the bladder and released when a person goes to the bathroom

vitamins group of substances we need to be healthy

whole-grain cereal grain that did not have the bran and embryo removed when it was processed

FINDING OUT MORE

BOOKS

Bean, Anita. *The Complete Guide to Sports Nutrition*. Guilford, Conn.:
Lyons, 2004.

Body Needs series: Titles include *Carbohydrates for a Healthy Body*, *Fats
for a Healthy Body*, *Proteins for a Healthy Body*, *Vitamins and Minerals
for a Healthy Body*, and *Water and Fiber for a Healthy Body*. Chicago:
Heinemann Library, 2003. This series looks at what the human body needs
to function healthily.

Davidson, Alan. *Penguin Companion to Food*. New York: Penguin, 2002.

Gifford, Clive. *Face the Facts: Drugs and Sports*. Chicago:
Heinemann Library, 2004.

Kedge, Joanna, and Joanna Watson. *Teen Issues: Diet*. Chicago: Raintree,
2005.

Levinson, David, and Karen Christensen. *Encyclopedia of World Sport*.
New York: Oxford University Press, 1999.

The Making of a Champion series: Titles include *A World-Class Mountain
Biker*, *A World-Class Gymnast*, and *A World-Class Sprinter*.
Chicago: Heinemann Library, 2004.

The Olympics series: Titles include *Ancient Olympics* and *Modern
Olympics*. Chicago: Heinemann Library, 2004.

FURTHER RESEARCH

If you are interested in finding out more about sports or nutrition, try
researching the following topics:

- The training and preparation needed to become a world-class athlete
- The history of the Olympics, including the ancient games at Olympia
  and the modern games since 1896
- How athletes are tested for drugs and the banned substances
  they need to avoid
- Fitness and diet for individual sports (governing bodies of sports
  usually give advice on their websites)
- Preparing for winter sports (especially the Winter Olympics).

WEBSITES

www.usda.gov

This is the site of the U.S. Department of Agriculture (USDA), which is responsible for food and nutrition in the United States.

www.fda.gov

This is the site of the U.S. Food and Drug Administration, an agency of the U.S. Department of Health and Human Services.

www.fitness.gov

This is the website for the President's Council on Physical Fitness and Sports.

www.nationaleatingdisorders.org

This is the website of the National Eating Disorders Association. This site lists different programs, books, and phone numbers you can look into to get advice or help.

www.iaaf.org

This is the website of the International Association of Athletics Federations (IAAF). It offers lots of information if you want to research world records, rankings, and more.

www.olympic.org

This is the official website of the Olympic Movement. It has information on different sports and athletes as well as links to all the international sports federations.

www.ussoccerplayers.com

This is the official website of the U.S. National Soccer Team Players Association.

www.sportsci.org

This Sports Science website offers information on sports medicine, nutrition, and the latest medical research.

INDEX